Email: books@brightersteppings.co.uk

Website: www.lifeatschool.org.uk

Author: Young Authors of Brighter Steppings

Publisher: Brighter Steppings Ltd

Cover Design, layout and illustrations: Elena Sevil

Distributed by: Brighter Steppings Ltd

Paperback ISBN: 978-0-9926076-0-9

Carl,

thanks for believing...

Seun & Arinola

Dedication

Dedicated to anyone that's been young once.

Acknowledgement

We would like to thank Barking & Dagenham Council community cohesion team for giving us the start up fund to write this book.

We would like to thank Vince Thomas, Angelica Gedviliene and the rest of the amazing Dagenham library team for providing ongoing in-kind support.

We would like to thank Arinola Araba for being such a walking heart throughout the process of writing and publishing this book.

We would like to thank Bullying UK (Family Lives) for granting us permission to use their contents on combating bullying.

We would like to thank Flora Kiakia, Celine Conte, Lorena Reigosa, Faisal Baig, Olga Biegus, Crystal Debrah, Starting Point, Anne Stairmand, Lara Popoola, Ayoola Champion for all the amazing supports and contributions.

As the young authors, we would like to thank our parents and guardians for their strong support and encouragements.

We would like to thank all those interviewed – Agni, Hannah Sansom, Karla, Ayobami Salami, Megan, Sharnakay, Vianni, Enoch Asekomhe, Brandon, Bonnie Stevens and everyone else.

We would also like to thank Elena Sevil for designing the illustrations, layout and cover for this book and Brighter Steppings Ltd for publishing our book.

Finally we would like to thank Seun Oshinaike for managing Life @ School.

To those whose names may not be mentioned, you are not forgotten, we are very grateful.

Young authors of Brighter Steppings:

Aderonke Adesanoye
Angel Sado
Benedicte Mbeka
Brandon Mbwese
Chloe King
Deborah Tshizungu
Ellie Ashton
Elizabeth Olabode
Eyram Kiakia
Giffty Nwabueze
Habeeb Ladipo
Jade Mahoney
Kany Kiakia
Korede Salami
Moriah St.Luce
Nana Aduse-Poku
Natalie Scowen
Saphy Nkopi
Shannon Leigh Adamberry
Shanelle Inico
Tyrese

Chapters

Hey! You have to read me first...
As you read through this book, tick the boxes of the best quotes you like and understand.
You can share your best quotes with us on our website at www.lifeatschool.org.uk
#LifeAtSchoolBestQuote

We have included 3D animations, which can be seen with most smartphones. What makes it cool is that when you download Aurasma app on your smartphone and place the phone on pages where you see this image that page will come to life on your phone.

Chapter 1

Life @ school

Starting secondary school

Starting secondary school can be a very exciting time, but not for all.

Some students feel nervous, scared or have mixed emotions. This is perfectly normal because almost every student has some hesitation towards secondary school.

What are your feelings about Year 7?

Daily routine at school

In secondary school you have a very regular routine, which can be very different to some primary schools. On average, most lessons are 1 hour each, with five lessons each day. This may seem very long, but you still have your breaks and lunches!

What you should look most forward to when going to school?

School has enjoyable parts, but can also be boring at times.

"You miss the 100% shots you don't take"
Wayne Grezky

School is a great place to meet your friends and hang out, but you still have to learn! Just remember to try hard in all lessons.

There are many things to look forward to.

Describe what your ideal school would look like?

What you should least look forward to when going to school?

We don't know about you, but school is not a reason for us to be happy when we wake up! Sometimes we may have to give in homework that we haven't done! Or, have a lesson with a really strict teacher, who can also be quite scary.

List what you don't like about school

The most important things about school

Depending on the person you ask; education is the most important part of school. There are still many people that disagree with this though. Others may think that the most important part of school is socializing and learning different skills.

What do you think is the most important?

☐ "Nothing is impossible, the word itself says 'I'm possible'!"

Audrey Hepburn

Chapter 2

Adventures at school

The most interesting things that has happened in school

We went on a School trip to France and Spain for three days and had to stop at different hotels, Disney land and Barcelona stadium, the only bad thing was we had a twenty-hour journey on the coach back home!

My group stayed at school to help organise a school disco.

One time I was a school councillor, and I was talking to the MP!

I've never received any award in my life and that was my first time to receive an award for something that I'd really done.

What interesting experience would you like in school?

Interesting opportunities we wish we had taken

I wish I joined more teams and different events in school.

I wish I was more focused on Geography, because I could've gone to Finland.

Going on different trips abroad; a ski trip to America and a netball trip to Spain.

"You are never too old to set another goal or to dream a new dream"

C. S. Lewis

#Iwish

I wish I had gone on the Malaysia trip, but I was told it is scary because you have to climb a mountain, and I don't want to die.

What opportunities would you like?

☐ "Change your thoughts and you change your world."

Norman Vincent Peale

Chapter 3

Music activities in school

Deciding the best music club or instrument to learn

When I did music I tried all the instruments. I tried the guitar but I couldn't play it then I tried the bass, I couldn't do it, but then I played the drum and I could play it.

You go to the music presentation and go through the entire musical instrument options.

You see your passion for it, and you can carry on learning it.

Pick the one that is best for you.

The benefits of being involved in musical activities

You meet new people and you learn how to play musical instruments and it opens new opportunities for your talent.

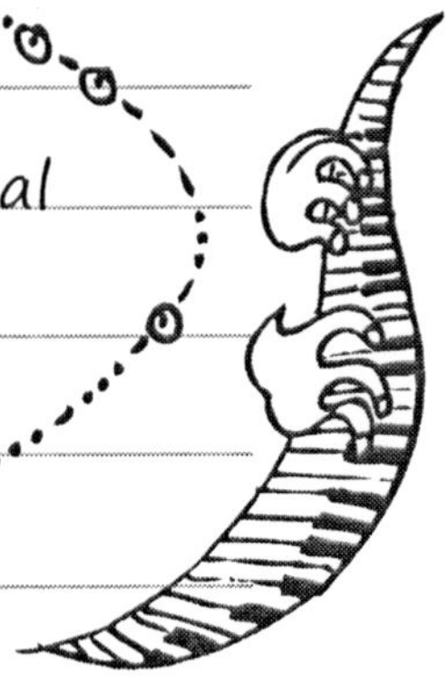

You can learn a new instrument which can help you in the future to get into university or college. Others might not play that instrument and you are one step above them.

Have funny experiences and gain confidence.

Sometimes you miss a bit of lesson time, other times you get to star in school concerts and go away to other schools to perform and places to perform. If you learn an instrument throughout your whole life, you might find a good job as a musician when you are older.

You get to show off!

"Our greatest weakness lies in giving up. The most certain way to succeed is always to try just one more time"
Thomas A. Edison

You can get to meet other people who share the same interest as you do and it can improve your chances of getting a job when your older. Someone got a job because they knew how to play the French horn.

There is the benefit of being in the orchestra and being in the winter show. There are a lot of performance shows, and you get to travel or even perform for the Royal family.

What musical instruments would you like to learn?

Chapter 4

Funny experiences

Funniest things that happened in school

I came out of P.E and there was a tissue stuck on my foot and I walked all the way to the playground with it!

It was in assembly when my teacher fell over and everyone laughed.

"Act as if what you do makes a difference. It does"
William James

Well, I have this tongue trick that I can do. In Year 7 that's how I was known in school; people took me about in school and showed everyone what I can do with my tongue.

It was our year photo and then everyone was standing on the year stand and my friend fell, it was really funny.

Teachers did their own adaptation video on a popular song, and they all looked silly.

I think it was food science: everyone had flour in a bag, and all of a sudden it turned into an egg and flour fight!

Some girl stole the teacher's lunch and hid it and made a map for him to find his soup. We put it in another class, and the door was locked, only he could see it. It was funny because he was hungry.

"Nothing great was ever achieved without enthusiasm"
Ralph Waldo Emerson

At Christmas all the teachers did this great big concert, you could see them all singing and acting like kids.

Share the funniest experience you can remember:

"Don't wait for extraordinary opportunities. Seize common occasions and make them great"
Orison Swett Marden

The funniest teachers in school

I've got two, Mr. Cabin, because he thought he could relate with the students, he used to make everyone laugh.
Ms Sprout, again she thought she could relate with the kids, and acts like she's one of us.

There's a teacher with a big beard and all the other teachers make fun of him.

I have to say Ms slanti who was walking down the corridor and fell flat on her face.

Who were the funniest teachers in your school?

☐ "Careful thinking and hard work will solve nearly all your problems. Try and see for yourself"
Ullery

Have fun!

Chapter 5

Sport activities in school

The best ways to get involved in sports clubs in school

- Go to the P.E department! There's always a big board with all the sports on it. You look on there and it shows all the events you can join.

- If you see sports activities you are interested in, go with someone who is interested as well- so you have a friend.
- You have to like the sport. If you don't like it, there is no point in getting involved, and it might be good getting a friend to come with you.

- You might be discouraged if there are people going whom you don't really know; but it's good for making new friends.

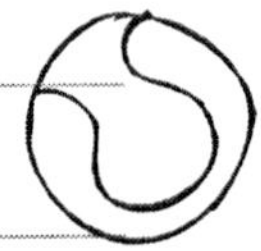

How many times have you played in a sport against the teachers?

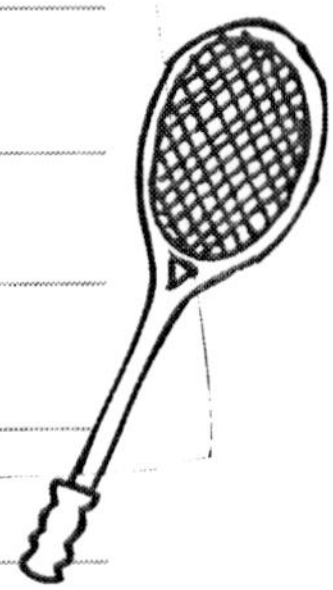

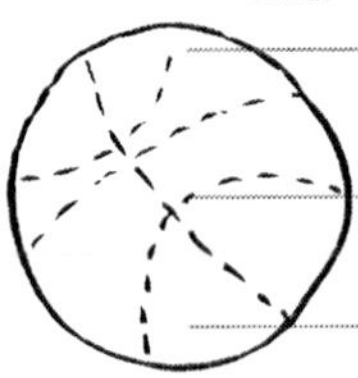

"Set your goals high, and don't stop till you get there"
Bo Jackson

Chapter 6

Personal School stories

Describe your most challenging day in year 7

I think it was the first day, I was the only person from my primary school except another person called Jacob; but I didn't want to hang out with him. He was crazy, even though he was funny; the first day it was easy because everybody wanted to make friends.

#myschoolstory

Going assembly for the first time and laughing my head off.

Making new friends was quite hard.

When I really had to poo and the toilets were filled up and I had to use the disabled toilet. While my best friend had to guard the door.

What have you found challenging in your life?

Make friends!

When we had to create a circle and say our names to each other, I was quite shy and nervous to meet everyone.

We had to find our classes, and some students gave us the wrong directions which just didn't make sense, so we got lost.

My most challenging day had to be the first day. You don't really know a lot of people, you have to go and explore.

Be brave!

The first day in school because I didn't know where anything was, it was awkward.

Can you imagine your first day at secondary school?

☐ "There is nothing to fear but fear itself"
Franklin D. Roosevelt

Steps to Making Long Lasting New Friends

1. Don't pick someone who will get you in trouble, pick someone who you think you will get along with, or has the same interest as you.

2. Walk up to them and say 'hi', and introduce yourself and be kind.

3. Start a conversation with a topic that interests you both.

4. As the conversation goes on you become more comfortable but make sure you are making the person feel comfortable too.

5. As long as you're yourself, people will accept who you are and from there, this may lead to a good friendship.

Be Kind!

You don't only have to talk to people who you think you would get along with. You can always be kind and talk to those who seem lonely because they have no one to talk to.

"What you do today can improve all your tomorrows"
Ralph Marston

Balancing school work, family and friends

Leave family issues at home.

Use certain days to do homework; it doesn't take that long, after you've done it, you have time to do everything else.

You have to be serious in class, and at lunch time you can make times for your friends and at home you can make time for your family.

Family comes first because they are the ones we have to wake up to in the morning and be terrified of. Homework comes second because it's our education, but friends come last because they can come, go and disappear when they want.

It's just about your priorities and what's more important to you.

Make a list of the best pranks you can think of

Chapter 7

Girls & Boys Experiences

Ideas on how to dress in school

If you're a girl, dress smartly to school and don't overdo it, don't think you have to put a lot of makeup on and wear the shortest skirt in the world to fit in. Some girls wear so much hairspray it looks like they've exploded. You need to calm down; it's not a disco. Just be your natural self.

A boy should dress smartly, with hair done and don't dress with trousers down to your knees, you know, not like a pimp basically.

No short skirts up to your thighs. Try not to be scruffy, people will think you are unhygienic or you're a dirty person. No ripped tights, if you have ripped tights take them off and borrow socks.

How would you be dressing to school?

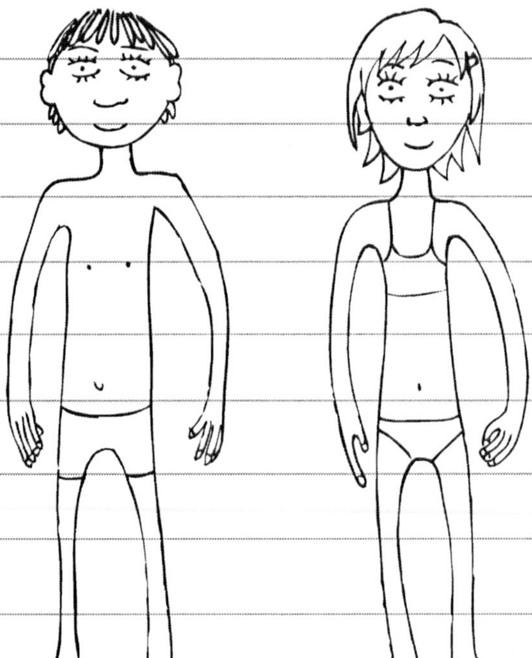

Being yourself in school

"You should be yourself, if you are not yourself you will pretend to be someone you're not."

Be yourself!

"Being yourself is important otherwise no one will know the real you, and the people who are your friends are not really your friends."

"Being you is the most important, being someone else won't help."

"I've learned that people will forget what you said, people will forget what you did, but people will never forget how you made them feel."
Maya Angelou

How school is different for girls than boys

Girls get judged more on their school uniform and looks and boys get judged on their behaviour.

Boys are not as interesting as girls, but boys have to remember they have to keep their pants up.

Girls have a lot of pressure and are often thought of as being smarter than boys. That's not always the case, but there's a lot of pressure on them to concentrate and be normal.

Some girls are different, they have different personalities. They are quiet and they do listen in class, overall there isn't much difference.

"Careful thinking and hard work will solve nearly all your problems. Try and see for yourself"
Ullery

Chapter 8
Annoying teachers

Experiences with annoying teachers

You will know when some teachers don't like you, they will make up reasons to get you into trouble or will shout at you for arguing back.
Well you shouldn't argue back!

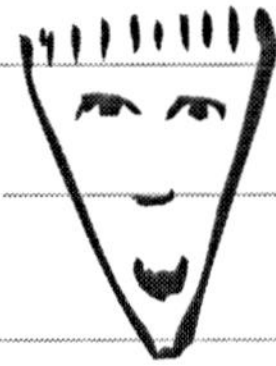

I had a crazy experience with a teacher; she started swearing at me! When teachers act like that you should tell your head of department. A school is a place where you need to feel comfortable.

A teacher used to ask all my friends if I was being good, and the teacher would say to my friends not to hang out with me because I can influence people.

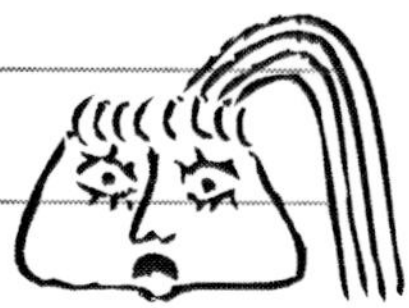

The most annoying teacher I know talks to me like I am five years old. She would talk to me very slowly and nodding her head like I'm five.

My art teacher, he is also my uncle-in-law, he just ends up going on about his villa in Spain, and we end up learning absolutely nothing.

The head of year in my school, she is unusual. I can tell she is a nice person, she cares about our opinion but she's a bit freaky and she doesn't pronounce my name properly.

What type of teacher would you be, if you were a teacher?

Coping with annoying teachers

"Don't talk back, tell your form tutor, or raise a complaint with the head teacher"

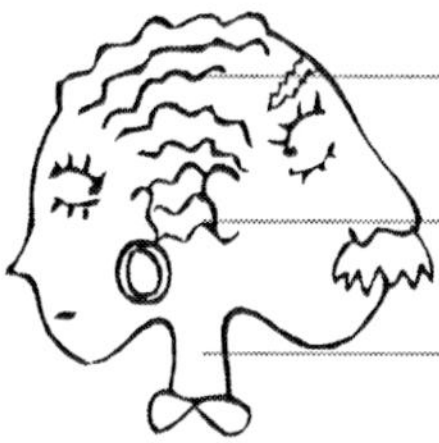

"Just don't do the things they don't want you to do"

"React in a positive manner because at the end of the day, there's not really much you can do about it. It's going to take a lot for them to lose their job because of one situation. At the end of the day they are teachers, you're meant to be there to learn"

"Make some effort to develop a good relationship with your teachers"

Were you ever scared of any of your teachers?

In year 7 I used to be scared of a teacher; she was scary as she'd shout all the time, and give us bad looks.

I was scared of my maths teacher; she'd threaten to call my parents.

I do think there's not really a good reason to be scared of a teacher, they are there to help you.

Describe your scariest teacher:

Chapter 9

Behaviour (Messing around in class, detention)

How to be funny but not getting in trouble in school

Think about the audience and think about the people around you, for example, if there's a big person in your class and you are making fun of weight don't do that, the student can be offended and feel bullied.

When you say something it should be a side comment, the teachers would hear it but it wouldn't be rude.

Just pretend like you are doing the work, and the person next to you will get into trouble. Not the best advice but it actually works!

Without making rude comments pick the right time and right audience for your jokes. You can joke with the teachers if you know they're up for it, but you don't have to make a big deal or a scene out of it.

Whenever its lunch time or break time, just talk to your friends and be a comedian but don't be a comedian in class not everyone is a comedian.

"Always desire to learn something useful"
Sophocles

"Optimism is the faith that leads to achievement. Nothing can be done without hope and confidence"
Helen Keller

To be funny or not to be!
That is the dilemma

When someone hurts another person you shouldn't be laughing, it's not funny.

You can tell what is a serious matter because when someone has a personal issue or disability, you don't joke about, ask yourself: how would I feel if it was you in that situation?

When to be funny is most probably lunch time and break time, or a lesson that a teacher gives you the chance to talk to your friends. You should always be serious in a test or in a lesson, and sometimes assemblies.

Don't be funny when you are meant to be revising for assessments, and when the teacher is preparing you for the next lesson which could be very important for your learning.

We have our serious times and our funny times. We need to pick the right moment, if you pick the wrong moment you will end up in trouble.

But if you're going to be silly, be silly in your own time...

Avoiding school detention

"Don't be... sneaky or annoy teachers and definitely stay out of teacher's way."

"Behave how the teacher wants you to and avoid doing things that will get you into trouble."

"Hand in homework on time, you have to listen in lesson and don't do other stuff when the teacher is talking. You have to apply yourself and don't fall behind with school work."

"If you feel a teacher is going to give you detention when you're arguing, then you might want to stop."

"Avoid detention by simply following, the code of conduct, simple rules you have to obey, no chewing gum in lessons, don't go in the science lab without the teachers permission."

"Some students can't avoid detention, it's not always easy, as no one is perfect."

"Things do not happen.
Things are made to happen"
John F. Kennedy

What did you do to get a detention?

Three times: once for lateness when I went to the shop to get chocolates and the other one was for homework.

I chatted back to most of my teachers when I was in Year 7.

Flicking a piece of foil and my phone went off, Blackberry's are stupid.

"Perseverance is failing 19 times and succeeding the 20th"
Julie Andrews ☐

To be honest, I have been in plenty of detentions: most of them was because I was distracted or talking, or laughing or cracking jokes.

Forgetting my kit for P.E.

You get at least one detention when you are in secondary school, you always have that one strict teacher who likes to give it for fun; but it's for your own good.

Chapter 10

How to stand out

How do students become the well known student in school?

"If you are nice and kind to everyone regardless of what they look like, that's how you will attract friends."

"Just be friends with everyone and everyone will know you. Pick out something your good at and everyone will know you for that."

"Be yourself, be true, be loyal and be friendly."

Who are the famous people you would like to be like?

How do you avoid being friends with the bad students?

"Just use your common sense and if you see a student doing bad things, you don't be their friend"

"If a student does something bad and you are aware of it why would you want to involve yourself with people like that?"

"Don't associate yourself with bad students. You have to respect your own choices for them to respect your choice"

"Though sometimes bad students are not bad kids; they just do the wrong things other kids avoid. So if they tell you to do something, don't do it"

Making friends with the well known students without changing yourself

Go up to the student and be yourself, if the student doesn't like who you are, there is no point in getting to know the student I guess.

You can make friends with one well known student and you will start getting more popular, but thennn! You're not in school education for that.

Some students believe there is no such thing as well known students, they are just known because they have big personalities. So it really depends on how big you want to expand your personality.

#makingfriends

What the well known students are like in school

You will find some well known students that are very big-headed, and they treat people like they are nothing but that's not all of them.

Well known students often have a very big group. Most of them are like really funny and really nice but some of them aren't. They are the type of people who like to joke around.

Chapter 11

Making friends

How do you make long lasting new friends? Gooood question!

Sometimes it starts from a point when you know someone from a long period of time. You build up a relationship and you trust each other, but below are different ideas.

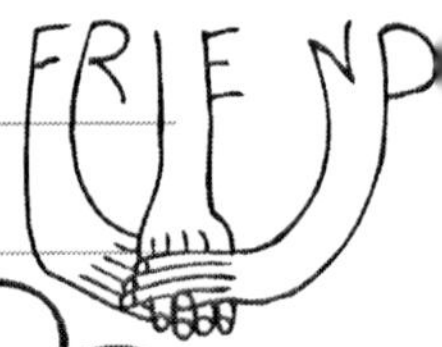

Smile, say 'hello', offer those lovely crisps and biscuits you have.

You have to always be kind to friends, joke with them and don't be shy.

Don't be different around your friend when you are in bigger groups.

Choose friends that you are happy with, and friends that accept you for who you are and never want to change you, friends that you are comfortable with.

The friends you want to know are the ones who stick by you, and they don't listen to the silly rumours about you. It doesn't happen straight away so it might take some time to build trust.

Which famous person would you like to be best friends with?

How to be a good friend to others

If a friend shares a secret with you, keep it. Respect their personal space and don't talk behind a friend's back, respect your friend as a person.

Always be reliable and trustworthy and don't let friends down. If you have an argument put it in the past.

#goodfriends

If your friend is being bullied you should stand up for them, don't just stand there, if they're upset, ask them what's wrong all the time.

What goes around comes around; treat people the same way you want to be treated.

☐ "With the new day comes new strength and new thoughts" Eleanor Roosevelt

Why some students find it hard to make good friends

"Some are shy and they don't want to talk to other students, so they won't be able to have any good friends."

"Often pretend to be someone they're not, and they often lie a lot."

"Some people just don't know when to take things serious, or be there for their friends, they just like to argue."

"Some students think they won't fit in with anyone."

Now you know some things to avoid! Don't miss out on that good friend.

What friends argue and fight about

"Petty things, if my friend doesn't like my hair we will argue."

"Why are you ignoring me? Why are you sad, why are you not talking to me? All the small stuff."

"Penny dropping on the floor, friend moaned and said it was her penny."

"Often about food, some people are gree-dy and it's good to share."

"Boys, copying what each other are wea-ring whatever is in fashion."

What do your friends argue about?

"We can't help everyone, but everyone can help someone"
Ronald Reagan

Keeping in touch with all the friends from primary school

You communicate with friends through the phone and social media most of the time.

It's really hard because you can only see them during the weekends, and talk to them on your phone or Internet.

Invent the best technology to keep in touch with friends

"The key is to keep company only with people who uplift you, whose presence calls forth your best"

Epictetus

How can I stop getting bullied?

You can tell a teacher. If you don't want to tell a teacher, tell your mum. If you decide to keep it to yourself, that isn't going to help.

If you're getting bullied, try and laugh with them because sometimes students don't mean to upset you. They're just trying to have a joke and if you prove to them that you don't care about what they are saying, they might not bother you anymore.

"Even if you fall on your face, you're still moving forward"
Victor Kiam

Chapter 12
Liz and bullying stories

I can't face school because of the bullies

Dear Liz,

I'm 14 and I can't face school any more. I want to move to a new one because it can't be any worse than this. I'm always on my own at break and I've got nobody to go around with. I've fallen out with my friends and they're going around with someone who used to bully me.

REPLY

I can understand why you're so unhappy but there may be ways this can be sorted out.

Moving to a new school isn't all that easy because the best ones are usually full and you may not get a place. You might end up at a less popular school which is further away from where you live and it can be hard to settle in when everyone else already has friends. It's also possible the bullies will have friends at the new school too.

These people who used to be your friends probably still like you in the same way, but they could be worried that if they show they still like you, that they'll get bullied in the same way.

One thing you could do is have a word with each of them individually, at a time when nobody else is around, and just sound them out. You could try to get them into conversation about something like what they did at the weekend and then just say that you used to be friends with them and you're not sure why that changed.

To have friends you also need to be a friend and you can do that by trying to be open and friendly with people and asking how they are.

"The capacity of young people to persevere, even under the most adverse conditions, never ceases to amaze me"
Jane Fonda

This isn't always easy because sometimes the people you are nice to aren't nice back, but if you just ask someone if they had a nice weekend then it gives them the chance to say something back and then you can try to continue the conversation.

People love talking about themselves, so in time, you will find people who like doing that because you'll come across as a good listener. Then people will enjoy your company and you'll find you have the same interests as some of them, which is the first step towards genuine friendship.

Liz

you are NEVER alone

Everyone has seen this horrible website which insults me

Dear Liz,

There's a website everyone at school knows about where people have been posting insulting messages about me, giving my name and also my school and the year I'm in. Lots of vile and untrue things have been said about me, and I don't know what to do. My mum wants to get the police involved but I'm afraid it will make things worse. I don't know who is behind it or how to complain and get the postings removed.

REPLY

I can understand why you're so upset about this, Bullying UK has closed down several of these unpleasant websites inviting others to post abuse.

Although this board has been set up by people who live in your area, it is hosted abroad. If you go to the 'help' menu on the board it should give you information about what to do if you have a complaint.

Ask your parents to send an email to the contact address explaining that abusive remarks are being made about you and that these almost certainly contravene the terms and conditions the message board owner signed when he took up the service.

Your parents should ask if all abusive messages about you and anyone else can be removed. They can explain that if there are a number of them they may amount to harassment under UK law and that they will be making a complaint to the police if they are not removed.

I'd also suggest that your parents alert your head teacher to this problem as you are probably not the only person being targeted in this way. If people are using school computers to upload this abuse then the school should be able to halt their internet use.

Liz

"It's easy to say young people should believe in themselves, but the number one thing is recognizing that it's a journey, that you have to build confidence in yourself"
Andrew Shue

Help me avoid bullies in the playground

Dear Liz,

I'm 9 and at primary school. When I'm playing football I get tripped up and they are always pushing me around and taking my dinner money. I often tell teachers about it because I've had a few injuries.

REPLY

I think you need to have some tactics to avoid problems. Stick to areas of school which you know are patrolled by staff because bullies are less likely to strike if there are a lot of people around.

Ask your mum or dad to write to your head teacher to outline what's been going on. Perhaps they could suggest that supervision is stepped up in the playground and that dinner money is handed in at the beginning of the day to be kept in a safe place.

Liz

People call me names because I'm a different colour

Dear Liz,

I go to a school with not many pupils from different backgrounds so I stand out. I'm often called names, jokes are told about me and I'm told to go back to where I came from but this is my home and I was born here. My family don't know what's being said to me and I don't want to upset them by telling them. They don't speak English very well and they might not be able to sort it out for me.

REPLY

If these ignorant people are making nasty remarks about your background, colour and culture then this is racism. Try having a word with your class teacher at a time he or she isn't busy. Perhaps you could tell other people you've forgotten to hand in your homework and have to stay behind to finish it.

If that doesn't work then your parents need to write to the head to explain the background and to ask for the name calling and jokes to be stopped.

If your parents find writing a letter difficult there may be someone in your community who would be able to help them.

Many towns also have Race Equality Councils and those are also places where they can find help.

Racism is serious and needs to be tackled. Many police forces now have special sections specifically to deal with this problem and if your parents need to contact them they should find someone understanding. Many forces also have police-school liaison officers who can be very useful in warning the bullies off.

Liz

I've seen bullies hurt a boy and I don't know what to do

Dear Liz,

There are a couple of bullies in my school who are bullying another boy. I feel very sorry for him. He doesn't tell anyone. They steal his money and make him cry. Once they got his glasses and smashed them and threw them in the toilet. Is there anything I can do to put a stop to this? I don't want to get on the bullies bad side either.

REPLY

It's kind of you to want to help this boy, he must be terribly upset. Could you be his friend to start with, it sounds as though he needs one?

Would you be able to tell his mum what has been happening because she needs to go into school about it? If you could discreetly tell a teacher that would be a good idea but don't get into difficulty with the bullies yourself.

What about going to the school office to borrow some cellotape, or a pen, and then quietly mentioning it to the school secretary?

Liz

People take the mick out of my illness

Dear Liz, A few years ago I was diagnosed with diabetes. Most of my friends are all right about it but some of them still take the mick. It can be upsetting, what can I do about it?

REPLY

It must be hard when people make fun over something which you can't help. I think there might be some mileage to be had about your heroism in having to test your blood every day. You could always say you'll give them a demo of pricking your finger to get blood out of it.

My guess is that they'd suddenly find they had somewhere else they needed to be – urgently!

If you have health and personal education classes, perhaps you or your parents could have a word with the teacher and a couple of sessions could be devoted to things like eczema, diabetes and asthma and how people control them. My guess is that half the class has got an inhaler stuffed away in a bag and once people understand more about conditions like these they're less likely to make fun of them.

Liz

"Sometimes, you follow your dreams. I say to the young people, 'If you have a dream, chase it'"
Karl Malone

People are bullying me on the school bus

Dear Liz,

There's a lot of fighting on my school bus and there's an older boy who keeps calling me names and having a go at me. My mum says she can't keep leaving work early to pick me up but I'm afraid what might happen. I live quite a way from the bus stop and I keep thinking the bullies can get me on the way home too.

REPLY

Schools can take action over bullying on the school bus. Your parents need to write to the head teacher about this problem.

Your parents could also speak to the bus firm because if there's trouble and bad behaviour on the bus then the bus firm might be pleased to have an excuse to complain to the school. That would mean nobody would know you complained and a general telling off might curb the bully. Look after your personal safety when you get off the bus. If it's dark then stick to well lit areas. Your parents could ask the police where they could get a personal attack alarm if that would make you feel safer. If you feel unsafe then go to a shop and ask them if you can wait there while you phone your parents to collect you.

If the worst happens and you are assaulted by one of the bullies then tell your parents who should report it to the police. Many offices, shops and streets are covered by CCTV so the bullies could be caught on film.

Liz

"One thing young people have to always keep in mind when deciding what they want to do with their lives is, is it fun? Is it something that I'm interested in?

Is it something I enjoy?"

Bob Schieffer

Bullying makes me so upset I want to die

Dear Liz,

I'm 14 in March and I'm being bullied constantly. I've had people hitting me and yesterday I had to go to hospital because I thought I had a broken finger. Please help me. I'm sick to death and sometimes I feel like killing myself. I wish I was dead.

REPLY

I can see that things are really bad for you, but killing yourself isn't the answer. Bullying Online can help you to get things sorted out, it may take time, but it can be done.

Be Strong

This is not something you can sort out on your own because it's gone too far for that. Your parents need to contact your head teacher to tell them how unhappy you are and to get the bullying stopped. If they've already done this but it hasn't worked there are other avenues they can try like making a complaint to the governors and the local council.

As you've been assaulted and had to go to hospital your parents should think about calling the police in, particularly if there were any independent witnesses to what happened when you got hurt.

If you feel life isn't worth living please go back to see your doctor to explain how you feel. If you want to talk things through with someone on the phone you can call the Samaritans on 08457 90 90 90.

Liz

"Keep true to the dreams of your youth"
Friedrich Von Schiller

I'm very depressed and I've been self harming

Dear Liz,

My grades at school have gone right down and I'm bunking off when my mum's at work because I can't face all the lessons I have with the bullies. I'm being called names about my weight and I have nobody to go around with at break. When I sit down with my packed lunch the others get up and move away. I'm taking so much time off that my mum is going to find out soon. I've told my head of year and she spoke to them but they're still doing it. This is making me feel very depressed and I've self-harmed a few times.

REPLY

I can understand why you don't want to go to school but if you take time off then you're damaging your chances of doing well in exams and that might affect your future.

Your mum needs to know what's going on so that she can help to get this sorted out. Try to find a time when she isn't busy to tell her or if you can't do that have a word with a grandparent or another member of your family or close friend and ask them to help you explain what's going on.

As you've already told your head of year then your mum needs to write to the head teacher explaining what's been going on and asking what strategy he/she can introduce to deal with the problem. Self harming is very dangerous and can easily go wrong. Please talk your feelings over with your doctor because he/she will be able to help you.

Keep a diary of who does and says what because that can be useful for the school to see what's going on.

Liz

Will I be bullied more when I change school?

Dear Liz,

I've been having trouble with girls in my class in Year 6 for a long time and I'm worried it's going to get worse when we all move up to secondary school. I'm also afraid I'm going to get new bullies on to me too.

REPLY

It's natural to be worried and nervous about changing school because it can seem like a big step but your mum and dad can help you out with this.

They can contact the head of the first year at your new school in the term before you start there and explain your concerns. Most schools don't want you to have a bad start to your new school life so they may be happy to make sure that you're not in the same form as the bullies.

When term begins it may seem strange at first but everyone else will be new too. Try to invite as many new people home as you can so that you get the chance to make lots of new friends. Join a few clubs and societies if you can too because that's another way of making friends.

Bullies usually target people they know so it would be unlucky for you to be bullied by someone older who was a stranger but if you're worried about this then stay in busy areas of school where there are plenty of other people.

Liz

"We can't afford to throw any young people away"

Benjamin Carson

Threats from girl in my street

Dear Liz,

I'm aged 14 and I'm not getting bullied at school but I get threats from an older girl who goes to my school and who lives in my street. We used to be really friendly but we fell out. I get nasty calls on my phone and takeaways and taxis sent to our house. I know she and her friends are behind it because sometimes she's said things in the text messages that only she would know. Do you think the school will do anything about her if my mum complains?

REPLY

The police are the best people to help here. If you get any more offensive or threatening texts don't reply to them but save them and ask your parents to contact the police. Sending these sorts of messages can be two types of offence. They might contravene telecommunications law and if this is part of a campaign of problems the calls could also amount to harassment.

If your parents take your phone to the police they can find out from your mobile phone firm where the messages came from. It can be time consuming for the police to do this but if there are a lot of messages then it's worth asking them to put a stop to it. Another way to stop the problem is for you to change your mobile phone SIM card.

Liz

Chapter 13

I remember when....

... Being more mature, meeting new people and making new friends.

... I made my first best friend, she didn't have any friends, and I became friends with her. I made her feel happy and comfortable.

... I fell over in Year Seven in front of a guy who I liked and it was very embarrassing.

... I fell down for the first time in secondary school and there was a big group of girls and they all started laughing at me. I also remember when I did my PDA homework and I got a 6B and I was very proud of myself.

... I used to have a massive backpack in year seven and I got seat belted (seat belted is when someone pulls your bag and it rips).

... Getting angry easily, I don't like other people taking advantage of me, and I've learned to control my anger.

... During the summer holidays, the teachers took some of the good students to a trip, we had tickets to see an Olympic game, and I went with my best friend. We went to the Olympic game and this was an experience I would remember for the rest of my life. We got to support our country and see live athletics, and we had free food.

What can you remember about primary school?

Chapter 14
Things that you will experience in Year 7

"You will experience different teachers and personalities, hard work, and many tests. Concentration is going to be extremely difficult."

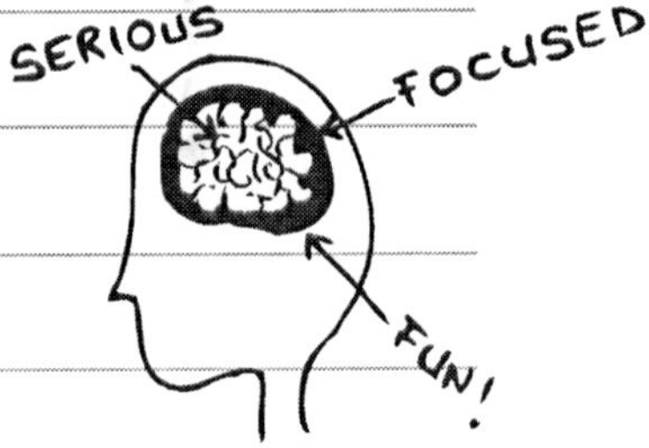

"Fun, teachers, food, friends, school work."

"You may feel lonely and confused; you are most likely to get into trouble, this is perfectly normal, because you have not adjusted yet."

"Everyone has been bullied, maybe not physically, expect it and don't let people hurt your confidence."

"There is an experience of becoming a better person, primary school is all laughs and jokes. Secondary school comes to real stuff, there is obviously getting to know new people, having to deal with more teachers and lots more work."

List 5 things you want to experience in Year 7

Chapter 15

Things to do for an hour every Sunday before school on Monday

What to do on Sunday:

- Check if you have done all your homework, check your planner and all your stuff in your bag
- Put your school things where you will remember them to avoid rushing on school mornings
- Make sure your school uniform is clean, try to eat and iron your clothes, sleep early
- Revision of your school work

Chapter 16

Things that clever students do in Year 7

A

Ask teacher for advice on how to improve yourself. Don't have detentions, expand on your answers, learn things outside school and join clubs.

Make sure your teachers know that you're clever, and they will treat you more special.

Generally be very polite.

Ask a lot of questions in class don't be too quiet, put in a lot of hard work, be persistent and don't give up.

Pay attention in class, don't get distracted, revise for tests, and get homework in on time.

Challenge and set targets for yourself.

Chapter 17

Things not to do

Don't go around like you own the school. Don't be rude to older kids. Try your best not to do any stupid things that will make a lot of people not like you, don't gain a bad reputation and don't be rude to teachers.

Don't give teachers a bad impression of yourself and make sure you have the right friends.

Don't be rude, and listen when the teacher is speaking, don't hang around the wrong crowd, focus in lesson.

Don't hate, judge, disrespect, and don't be a fake.

"I would so much like young people to have a sense of the gift that they are"
John Denver

Chapter 18

Things teachers dislike

- Rude students
- Not giving your homework on time
- Losing your books
- Making foolish jokes
- Loudness
- Talkative
- Failing to do what teachers know you are capable of and you choose not to do it
- Bullies
- Physical violence and backchat

Constantly coming late to lesson

Chapter 19

Things teachers like

- Smart children
- Not forgetting equipment
- Students who expand on their answers
- Raising hands in class
- Hardworking students
- Happy students
- Students who try their best
- Students who ask clever questions
- Doing your homework
- Students that get on well with others

Chapter 20

Things not to do in the play ground

- Don't do a stupid dare
- Don't start a fight for no reason
- Don't have a fight in the play ground, don't have water fights without the teacher's permission, don't throw stones and don't bully other students
- Pushing someone over, physical violence

- Fight or play fight

Chapter 21

Things not to do in the classroom in Year 7

Don't chew gum, don't put your feet on table, don't talk back, and don't make fun out of your teacher.

Do not drink without permission; never put your bag in the middle of the room, but seriously why would anyone want to do that?

Don't lie, don't always laugh at everyone and go with the crowd.

Running around in the classroom and throwing things at people.

If you're in a science lab don't even think of doing a crazy experiment, because you can harm others, and don't do anything you might regret.

Chapter 22

Things that make you a high grade student in Year 7

Doing all your homework; being hardworking, never giving up. Asking teachers questions if you don't understand something; and looking back at what you don't understand, doing your own research.

Always do extra revision at home and complete your homework inside and outside school. Always be polite to the teacher and discover more things.

Make sure you understand everything, if not just talk to your teacher, they can help you revise for tests.

Take pride in your work.

Aim high, set yourself targets and go far.

"When you are honest and open with young people, they let you in"
Magic Johnson

Chapter 23

Things young people should do during free time?

"Eat chicken, socialise, watch TV, read books, listen to music, act like a child, and don't act stupid."

"Play sports, hang out with your friends, and try making new friends."

"Have fun in the park and do your homework."

"Don't just sit in front of the TV or video games all your life, find activities and join sports groups or music groups."

"Spend time with yourself and spend time revising, things that help build you how you want to be."

"I think young people should have a lot of fun"
Syd Barrett